"In a time of staff shortages too often new staff are thrown into their position without much training and orientation to the position, company, and culture. To be successful, your company needs to have a plan for onboarding new staff, getting them up to speed and plugged in with your team. This book shows you how to have that success."

—**Mark Schinnerer**, Speaker, Success Coach, Award-Winning Author of *The Success Grower*

"Amanda Painter and Brenda Haire are absolute masters at demystifying and simplifying all things HR. *The Onboarding Process* is a complete and easy to implement roadmap for successfully integrating new hires into your company so they can flourish and thrive from the moment they become a part of your team. This series of books is brilliant and should be on the desk of every HR manager."

—**Joan Turley**, CEO and Founder, Salon & Spa Made Simple, Author of *Sacred Work in Secular Places*

"This book walks your team through the process of connecting your new hire to not only your team but also to the culture and systems you already have in place! If your team isn't connected internally, how can they connect with your clients? Get this book and help your team become better connected from day one!"

—**Chris Borja**, Founder, CONNECTED Networking Group and Become a Better Networker, CEO, Borja Virtual Conferences and Events

"I know firsthand the support entrepreneurs need. This series is the HR department you didn't know you needed. *The Onboarding Process* connects your new hire to your company through a clear step-by-step system that anyone can follow and is vital to your bottom line. Who you bring into your company and how you onboard them has a great impact on your current team. This book shows you how to do it the smart way."

—**Jacob WP Ramey**, CEO Platinum TDM

THE ONBOARDING PROCESS

HOW TO
CONNECT YOUR NEW HIRE

Other Books by the Authors

The Team Solution Series

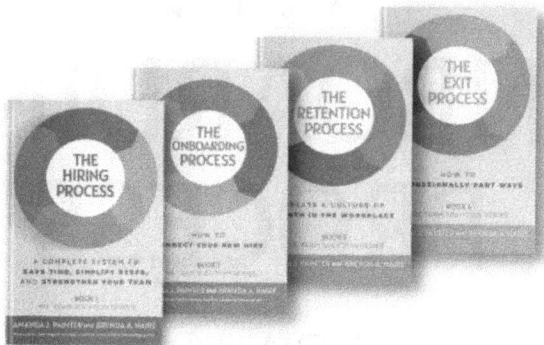

The Author Solution Series

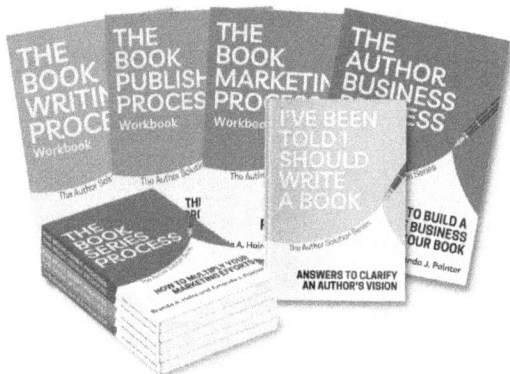

Also by Brenda A. Haire

TheJoyOfPursuit.com

THE ONBOARDING PROCESS

HOW TO
CONNECT YOUR NEW HIRE

AMANDA J. PAINTER
and
BRENDA A. HAIRE

BOOK 2
THE TEAM SOLUTION SERIES

Joy *of* PURSUIT
PUBLISHING

Published by Joy of Pursuit Publishing

Chandler, Texas 75758

JoyofPursuitPublishing.com

Library of Congress Cataloging: 2022935544

Softcover: 978-1-957205-80-9

Hardcover: 978-1-957205-03-8

E-book: 978-1-957205-04-5

Throughout the book, you'll be introduced to new tools. We provide examples, templates, checklists, worksheets, and more.

Download your free bundle at
theJoyOfPursuit.com/Onboarding

Disclaimer

The information shared in this book is meant to guide employers through the onboarding process. The content of this book is not meant to be a substitute for professional legal or tax advice. Given the nature of continually changing laws in the United States, it is advised that employers seek private legal resources and abide by their most current local and federal laws. Joy of Pursuit Publishing and the authors of this book are not responsible for any business's failure to comply with any local or federal law.

We realize this book will be distributed globally and that some of its contents will not be relevant to specific employment laws or regulations outside of the United States. Employers outside of the United States are advised to do their due diligence to follow all laws and regulations applicable to them. Joy of Pursuit Publishing and the authors of this book are not responsible for any business's failure to comply.

Dedication

To all the hopeful new hires, volunteers, contractors, and interns seeking a place in which to grow their grace-given gifts and careers. And to the teams welcoming them home.

Contents

Foreword

Do you remember your first day of work at a brand-new opportunity? I remember every single one: the butterflies, the unknown, the excitement and the thought, "Will this be a good fit for me?"

So much depended on the experience of onboarding. Interviews are like a dating relationship, which ultimately leads to agreeing to work with each other—the wedding day! Onboarding, then, is like the honeymoon. If THAT is disappointing or downright disastrous, how long do you think that marriage is going to last?

Carrying the analogy even further, if you view your company's clients as the children in this new marriage, how will a rocky, inconsistent relationship affect them?

You have greatly improved your hiring and interviewing process, thanks to Brenda and Amanda's book, *The Hiring Process.* This book is about the next step, which is equally as important.

The Onboarding Process provides the tools to create and sustain a positive, engaging onboarding experience. That American quick-service franchise we all know that serves sweet tea, waffle fries, and sandwiches made from chicken, you know the one, they obviously have an excellent system in place to onboard qualified candidates who are eager to work there.

Your company can generate the same kind of enthusiasm for new hires. Whether you are a startup (an ideal time to develop a strong onboarding approach) or an established business, the proven concepts in this book will ensure that you intentionally and thoroughly craft a magnetic onboarding experience. The word will get out, and your company will attract and keep the high-quality team members you need to provide a five-star customer experience.

Retention starts day one, not year one. That is way too late to discover that a team member is already heading out the door.

Amanda and Brenda's insights will encourage you if you are on the right track or making your processes even better. If your company is struggling with onboarding, this book will give you hope—you absolutely can turn things around. Onboarding can be improved anywhere along your team members' journeys with you. It's never too late to engage your team.

So, how do they accomplish this? I'm glad you asked! These authors have the knack of breaking down a big strategic goal into next best steps with tangible action items.

The Onboarding Process is Book 2 in *The Team Solution Series* that helps start any team member off on the right foot while protecting your existing team and processes.

Helping companies become heroes in every human interaction is vital to the long-term success of the company. With years of experience in the customer experience, I can't emphasize enough how important onboarding your team is and how it directly affects your profitability.

Client satisfaction is directly related to employee satisfaction. Starting a new employee off with proper expectations and understanding of the company's vision is wise. Creating a sound process so that your entire team is in alignment is genius. Thankfully, in this book, you get access to that genius and all the steps in the process. Do not neglect this often-overlooked aspect of hiring.

Building a team takes effort. Building a team committed to your goals and the work it will take to achieve them is only possible with systematic intentionality. Investing in this process is investing in your team and the future of your company.

Of course, it's not enough to just read this book. You'll have to apply the knowledge. This book should be read company wide. Everyone in your workplace should understand the value of welcoming new team members while keeping the culture they all enjoy.

John Maxwell wisely says, "Everything rises and falls on leadership." Complete buy-in to the onboarding experience must begin with those who lead. I highly recommend providing this book to your entire executive team and department heads, not just Human Resources or direct supervisors. Every single team member should read this book for your business to provide a stellar onboarding experience.

We've all heard about "The Great Resignation," as it's being called. Your company can stand far above other businesses in your area if you commit to making the honeymoon (onboarding) and marriage a spectacular success.

Read this book and apply its principles; you'll be glad you did!

John D. Hanson
President | Consultant | Speaker | Author
Accelerated Revenue Inc.
accrev.com/consulting/

A Note to You—the Reader

If you want to build a ship,
don't drum up people together
to collect wood and don't assign them
tasks and work, but rather teach them
to long for the endless immensity of the sea.

—Antoine de Saint-Exupéry

Congratulations on taking the necessary steps in setting up your onboarding process. This book will be your down-to-earth, step-by-step guide for what may seem like a complicated process to you now.

We recommend you chart your standard onboarding process *before* hiring anyone, and we intend this book to be your map. Read it thoroughly and keep it handy. By seeing the journey ahead of you, as well as your destination, you will be well prepared for your new hire, and the process won't be as intimidating.

(Throughout this book, we will refer to new hires but understand that this process can and should be adapted for department transfers, contractors, volunteers, and interns [whether paid or unpaid].)

The first book in *The Team Solution Series* —*The Hiring Process: A Complete System to Save Time, Simplify Steps, and Strengthen Your Team*—provides a guide for successful hiring. But a successful hiring process is only a first step toward having a successful team. The theme of excellent and straightforward communication from *The Hiring Process* carries through to this book as well.

Onboarding is the time to follow through with promises communicated during the recruitment and hiring process.

Don't allow onboarding to be an afterthought or rushed through. Take the time to be strategic when planning your onboarding process and ensure it is well executed. This process goes well beyond employee orientation. It's not handing a new hire a Team Handbook, playing a thirty-minute orientation video, and wishing them luck. Yes, orientation is important, but it is only one component of the overall onboarding process.

This process is extensive; it should last several months (we recommend ninety days) and will involve

Plan your onboarding process *before* hiring.

other team members as well. Invest in creating a quality system so it can be duplicated for all new hires. Your company will benefit in the long run.

New hires need the connections, tools, and resources to start off on the right foot and do their job well for years to come. Onboarding is the foundational piece of the employee experience.

Don't get overwhelmed if you are starting from scratch. A wide variety of proven tools and systems can be used for onboarding. You likely have some of these in place already. After reading this book, you can integrate anything currently working for you with our comprehensive but streamlined process. Some of the tools you may already have to incorporate into your onboarding process include:

- Website or digital storage
- Social media
- Explanatory or how-to videos
- Job shadowing
- Handbooks

An employee's first few days on the job will greatly influence how long they stay with your company. Inadequate onboarding can lead to subpar performance and lower retention. When onboarding is rushed or done poorly, employees will be confused, frustrated, and ill-prepared, and turnover will be greater. But when you communicate what success looks like and provide the tools and systems employees need to achieve that success, it leads to job satisfaction and creates long-term, loyal employees. This is why your onboarding process is crucial to employee retention.

Onboarding is a delicate balance between the need to quickly assimilate someone to the team and the necessary time to get them acquainted. It should prepare your new hire for excellence in all areas of your company, from company culture to policies and systems. While performance in any role is important, success includes a productive and happy work environment, thus making a productive and happy employee.

In the chapters that follow, we will walk you through the seven C's of onboarding:

- How to **collaborate** with your team for a fluid onboarding process
- What to **communicate** when and how
- Solutions to common onboarding **challenges**
- Details of **compliance** necessary to protect both your company and employees
- **Clarifying** expectations every step of the way for the new hire
- **Connecting** your new hire to the people and tools needed to succeed
- Strategies to integrate your new hire into your company **culture** and team

We understand that in today's workforce, many companies are moving to a hybrid work environment, and we will discuss how this affects onboarding throughout. There is a specific section on this in Chapter 2 as well. If at any point you need assistance in adapting your process from in person to online or hybrid, we'd be happy to consult with you and your team.

Chapter One

Collaboration and Communication

Collaboration is a key part of the success of any organization, executed through a clearly defined vision and mission and based on transparency and constant communication.

—Dinesh Paliwal

Team Collaboration

Collaboration is key to a cohesive team, and when done well, onboarding is a collaborative effort. As mentioned in *The Hiring Process,* hiring should be collaborative, and team effort should be sustained throughout onboarding. When crafting your onboarding process, don't try to do it alone or give the task to one person on your team. Your Leadership Team should work together to decide what the process looks like for your business. When created together, the plan is more likely to be comprehensive and applicable to the entire company.

Here are some questions to consider when creating your onboarding process:

- When does it start, and how long does it last?
- What impression do you want a new hire to have after their first day—Core Values, company culture, et cetera?
- Who is involved in the process—HR managers, leadership, Accounting, IT, co-workers, mentors?
- What goals will be set for the new employee?

- Where will your new hire go for help—training materials, a mentor, Team Handbook?
- How will you collect feedback to measure success or make improvements?

Beyond your Leadership Team, you will need to collaborate with all departments to make sure they are represented in the process. Do they have the tools they need and understand the strategy to ensure a smooth onboarding process? Create a clear hand-off schedule to utilize once a new hire is in place. This will allow each department to know who the new hire is meeting with next, who the point of contact is, and when they are meeting.

Everyone on your team, especially managers and supervisors who will work closest with new hires, must be accountable to the process. The most well-designed process is worthless if your team isn't going to implement it. This is why team collaboration is crucial. When given a voice in developing the process, your team will be more likely to understand its importance and ensure it is utilized in their department.

When designing a new onboarding process, or revamping an old one, ask recently hired individuals what they would like to see done differently compared to their onboarding. Feedback from those who have recently gone through the process will offer insight and a unique perspective. You can collaborate with these team members in a number of ways—a survey, one-on-one interviews, or group brainstorming sessions.

Team Communication

Onboarding isn't only about preparing your new hire to join the team; it's about preparing your team for the new hire, well before their first day. This is why team communication is essential. You never want someone on your team to say, "Who is this?" when meeting a new team member. That demonstrates a lack of consideration to your current team as well as the new hire.

An onboarding process should be in place in each company department—for new hires as well as departmental transfers. For clarity and consistency in this book, we will continue to refer to new hires, but you should set up a similar process for internal company transfers, volunteers, interns, and/or contractors.

Here are some items to consider when setting up onboarding for each department: (These may be different or need some adjustment depending on the size of your company.)

- Payroll/Accounting—tax forms and documents, 401(k), direct deposit and other payment methods, how and where to track hours
- HR/Compliance—oversees the onboarding   process,   legal   forms,

employee identification, insurance, updates the organizational chart and Team Directory (Make sure you've removed the public job posting. Review *The Hiring Process* Chapter 7 "Wrap-up and Resources" for more information on transitioning from one process to the next.)

- IT/Tech—email, devices, access codes and passwords, software, website updates
- Admin—orders supplies and business cards, prepares the workspace, creates a welcome package
- Facilities—new furniture, keys, access card, parking

The entire onboarding process is typically owned by someone in the HR department whose title may be Hiring Supervisor, Onboarding Specialist, or other. In this book, we will refer to this person as the Hiring Manager. If you are a small company and do not have a dedicated HR department, this may fall to someone in Finance, a member of your Leadership Team, or the supervisor who will directly oversee the new hire.

The Hiring Manager should announce the new hire to the entire team, including role, title, department, et cetera. Ask anyone who will work directly with the new hire to reach out individually and welcome them.

Also, select long-term team members or top performers to connect with the new hire.

Prepare your team for the new hire.

Think of the team members who exemplify all your Core Values. These are the people you want your new hire to create working relationships with and look to regarding company culture.

Have the appropriate department supervisors/directors organize a departmental meeting for face-to-face introductions, whether online or in person. Then work together to arrange cross-departmental meetings for key roles that integrate with the new hire's position. Create ways for social interaction and building connections. Integration into the team should be the top priority.

When it comes to firsthand interaction with your new hire, the two positions most involved during onboarding are the Hiring Manager and the new hire's direct supervisor.

Collaborate as a team to create an Onboarding Checklist to assist each of these roles with managing the process.

Integration into the team should be the top priority.

The *Company* Onboarding Checklist will be an overview of the company-wide process and utilized by the Hiring Manager. The department supervisor will use the *Department* Onboarding Checklist to ensure the new hire or transfer completes all onboarding tasks relevant to their department.

See examples here of both Onboarding Checklists and notice the differences between the overall company and the internal department perspectives.

Company Onboarding Checklist

- [ ] Send onboarding packet
  - [ ] Welcome letter
    - [ ] First-day information:
      - [ ] Location, time, and date
      - [ ] Where to park and entrance information
    - [ ] Dress code information
    - [ ] Reminder to bring picture ID for the first day
    - [ ] Contact information for Hiring Manager and direct supervisor: Name, email, phone number
  - [ ] Paperwork to complete electronically
  - [ ] Team Handbook
  - [ ] Company Directory
  - [ ] OAR Chart
  - [ ] First-Day Schedule

Coordinate with IT Department
- [ ] Email setup
- [ ] Software access
- [ ] Asset List (computer, badge, etc.)

Admin Tasks
- [ ] Update OAR Chart
- [ ] Update directory
- [ ] Add birthday to team calendar
- [ ] Order business cards
- [ ] Arrange welcome package

Communication
- [ ] Company wide announcement, including name, title, department, etc.
- [ ] Ask leadership team to send a welcome note
- [ ] Assign mentor and schedule first meeting

Department Checklist

- [ ] Send welcome note introducing yourself
- [ ] Ask others in the department to send a welcome note
- [ ] Provide access to
    - [ ] Team channel on communication platform
    - [ ] Team planning documents
    - [ ] Task lists in project management software
    - [ ] Calendar and department meeting schedule

Communications
- [ ] Schedule departmental meeting for face-to-face introductions.
- [ ] Arrange cross-departmental meetings for key roles that integrate with new hire.

Work with New Hire
- [ ] Review Job Description with new hire and discuss expectations.
- [ ] Schedule bookend meetings for first week.
- [ ] Share training materials for department processes.
- [ ] Schedule training sessions for specific needs.
- [ ] Discuss department goals.
- [ ] Complete Goal MAP.
- [ ] Schedule Onboarding Review.

At end of 90 days
- [ ] Complete Onboarding ScoreCARD.
- [ ] Conduct Onboarding Review.
- [ ] Collect Onboarding Feedback Form.

Early Onboarding

Now that your team is up to speed and notified of the new hire, you need to focus your communication on the new team member. First impressions are most important, which is why onboarding matters.

There will likely be a gap of time between when the job offer is accepted and the employee's first day. Make the most of this time.

It's a great opportunity to provide your new hire with more information **First impressions are most important.** about the company and begin to build a relationship with them. Keep them engaged. Set expectations and ease nerves. This will ensure they are ready for success when arriving on their first day.

New hires will be more likely to acclimate on their first day if they are prepared and have had time to review and absorb some information ahead of time. Be sure to highlight anything that is vital to their specific role. Bringing awareness to company history is important, but knowing how much the product they will be selling costs and the deliverables provided with it matters more in the day-to-day function of their role. Communicating this type of specific detail will set them up for success.

Send every new hire an onboarding packet. This may be digital or a physical package if applicable. Most of the packet will be the same for all new hires but take some time to customize it. Here is a list of what to include:

- Welcome letter tailored to them highlighting those role-specific items mentioned above. For example, "Be sure to check out page seven, which covers our products and services. This information will be helpful to you in the Sales Department." Also remind them about documents that they will need to provide (e.g., picture ID).

- Paperwork—We'll share more on this and other compliance items in Chapter 3.
- Team Handbook—Have you created one yet? We'll outline it for you in Chapter 3.
- Team Directory—How will they contact team members? See Chapter 5 for more information on directories.
- OAR (Organizational, Accountability, Responsibility) Chart—You can find more information on this in Chapter 5.
- First-day schedule—The first day can be exciting but also nerve-racking. Provide your new hire with a schedule showing what their first day (or week) will look like. More on this in Chapter 4.

Tip: Utilizing technology will streamline your early onboarding process. Send links to any forms that can be completed and submitted electronically. Communicate how to complete them and that you would like them submitted prior to their first day.

Early onboarding is also the perfect time to grant early access to communication platforms. This will allow your new hire to get their feet wet and remove some stress by connecting them to their new colleagues before they start. But if you do, communicate very specifically about what they are to do or see.

We once had a con-tractor, who wasn't well instructed by his supervisor, add himself **Communicate relevant and specific details.** to chat groups he had no business being in. Be specific. Don't make them guess what actions you want them to take. If inviting them to an online workspace, let them know what teams, channels, or projects they will be included in and if there is any action they need to take once they are in the group.

Share with the new hire any relevant contact information—their point of contact or who they will report to. This will likely be the Hiring Manager, who will guide them through onboarding, and their direct supervisor, who they will be accountable to.

The point is to help your new hire not feel as if they are walking in (or logging on) blind on their first day. The more comfortable and confident they are, the faster they will become productive. Think through all the ways you can make them feel like part of the team immediately. For example, if everyone wears a uniform or badge, have theirs prepared ahead of time so they don't feel out of place or stand out any more than they already will as the new hire. Alleviate some uncertainty by letting them know where to park and who to ask for upon arrival.

It all comes down to communication. Be intentional, clear, and specific in all the ways you communicate during early onboarding.

Chapter Two

Challenges

Talent is the multiplier.
The more energy and attention you invest in it,
the greater the yield.

—Marcus Buckingham

Prior Engagements

This is always an awkward topic for a new hire, but it is important for your team to know when someone will be out. Make it easy for your new hire by asking if they have any previous engagements, required absences, or vacations planned that should be added to the company or department calendar. Your HR Department should keep track of this information, but the new hire's specific department should be aware as well for planning purposes.

Relocation Struggles

If your new hire relocated to accept the position, keep this in mind during onboarding. Moving to a new city or state can be challenging, especially if their family or children are joining them. Provide additional relocation services and support for them. Take into consideration the time they need to unpack and settle into their new home. You can share a standard list of recommendations, such as realtors, restaurants, lawn services, utilities, et cetera. Think through specific needs for someone new to your area.

You could send a welcome basket to their new address with some locally themed items along with company swag. As with any swag, make it something useful and not random branded merchandise.

Too Much Information

Slowly drip your onboarding information rather than come at your new hire like a firehose. Starting a new position or transitioning in a company can be overwhelming enough. Don't go full blast only to realize your new hire has tuned out and is second-guessing their decision to work with you. Set a smooth professional tone, even if you work in a fast-paced environment. Too much too soon, and in too many ways, can be chaotic and create confusion.

Everyone processes information differently. You likely learned some of how your new hire processes information through the hiring process. Now, it's time to remember that not everyone learns the same way, and not all information is relevant to all departments and positions. This is why it is extremely important to collaborate with your team in creating your customized onboarding process.

It is better for the new hire to understand *where* to retrieve the

Too much too soon can create confusion.

information when the time comes to comprehend and implement it rather than give the false impression that they need to read and understand every detail of your operating procedures on day one. Reassure them that they will have continuous access to this information. Suggest they skim through to understand what is available so that when questions arise, they know where to get answers.

While it is important for every employee to know the company history, it may not be the first thing every department shares. As long as all the pertinent information is eventually covered and the Leadership Team agrees when during the ninety-day onboarding process the information is shared, let the new hire work at their own pace.

Customize for the Position

Work through the information your company deems necessary to share with all new hires, and then build each department onboarding process based on this foundation. Be sure you create a relevant onboarding experience for each new hire. Provide the right content for the specific role.

You'll read later in Chapter 4 about how orientation should be the same for everyone in the company. But the remainder of the onboarding should be customized. Don't fall into the trap of thinking it's a one-and-done process. The Hiring Manager will need to collaborate with each department supervisor to design customized training that is relevant to the position.

Transfers vs. Hires

Often someone transferring departments will miss departmental onboarding. Don't make assumptions about their knowledge or neglect the social aspects of transferring into a new position. Each department is unique.

Tips for departmental transfers:

1. Update the OAR Chart and make appropriate introductions. Change access to software, emails, projects, channels, etc.
2. Make sure your Accounting Department and the transfer are aware of any pay increase, if applicable, and when it will go into effect.
3. Provide the transfer with any training needed for this specific role. It is not likely that all procedures are the same for each department, including team communication, software, equipment, et cetera.

4. Allow opportunities for building relationships.

5. Don't assume that because the person has been with your company for any length of time they understand what other departments know or specialize in.

6. Look to *The Exit Process* for more information about transferring them out of their previous position and *The Hiring Process* for more information on creating a new open job posting.

Bad Hire/Bad Fit

Has it become evident that your new hire stretched the truth about their skills or experience? Maybe they don't see how their previous experience aligns with your product or service. They may have been a rock star computer sales rep, but now you're asking them to close $100,000 contracts, and they just can't perform at the level you need.

Here's a story a colleague once shared regarding a new hire. This individual was "highly recommended and perfect for the position," according to the company's owner/CEO. Due to this recommendation, the owner bypassed the established hiring process and hired her without proper vetting.

Within a couple of weeks, the new hire (who was working in the Finance Department) was tasked with sending a refund to a customer. While doing so, she had many questions, asked for extensive oversight, and eventually admitted that sending a refund and managing that amount of money "scared her." This should not have been the case for someone who was hired for this position. It became evident that even though she had some financial experience, she had none with the level of responsibility required for managing high-dollar contracts and transactions.

We never want to find ourselves in a position like this with a new hire, but it does happen.

Here are some solutions to apply to the situation:

- Further evaluate using a Skills Assessment and/or Capacity Check. (Get examples of these and other tools in *The Hiring Process* Toolbox.)
- Properly onboard for a ninety-day period from that point forward.
- Provide additional training on company specifics and requirements.
- Demote or limit responsibilities.
- Transfer to another position within the company.
- Fire.

We all make mistakes, which is why you should never burn a bridge with other candidates, as we suggested in *The Hiring Process*. This is also why your entire company must follow the process you have in place to safeguard from mistakes as much as possible. If you do have to let an employee go, regardless of circumstances, it is helpful to be able to access the list of original candidates and reassess to see if one of them is the right fit for the job.

If you are consistently seeing unqualified or inconsistent hires, it is time to revisit your hiring process. Take the time to reassess how you screen candidates and assess their skill sets. What is the missing or weak link in your system? Does your company even have a standard process in place? If you need more guidance on this topic, *The Hiring Process* provides all the tools needed to create and implement a strong hiring process.

Solutions to Remote Onboarding Challenges

Equipment and Environment

Equipment, Internet access, lighting, background, attire, quiet workspace—all these sound like the basics until someone doesn't understand their importance. Be sure there is a clear understanding of who is providing what and that this was communicated in the job posting, interviews, and job offer, as mentioned in *The Hiring Process.*

Communicate the environmental expectations of remote and online work. We have company expectations that team members' cameras remain on during online meetings. If face-to-face interaction is important to your company culture, make sure you communicate it. Brenda equates a disabled video to showing up in her office with a bag over your head. This would be unacceptable, so why would you allow your team to show up online the same way? It's especially inappropriate for client meetings. Set clear expectations and boundaries in your remote or hybrid workplace early.

Personalized Communication

Don't send a welcome email or interoffice communication that is simply cut and pasted from a template. Add warmth and personalization. Put effort into adding the hospitable emotion you would normally express when meeting in person. Remember, if you cut and paste the same interoffice communication used before, the last new hire may see it and recognize your insincerity, costing you credibility and authority.

Creative Introductions

Whereas relationship-building comes naturally when working in an office, leaders must be creative and think outside the box to recreate this in an online environment.

Schedule meet-and-greets, coffee chats, lunches, and other socialization times for your new hire. These can be hosted online if you're hybrid or remote and should be casual and comfortable. Don't put your new hire on the spot in front of six team members and say, "Tell us about yourself." Instead, spur the conversation to emerge organically.

For larger teams that need to move through the group conversation in a timely manner, use an easy icebreaker like "This or That?" or something similar. Let the group know you're going to use a fast icebreaker to get to know each other and your new hire a bit better and that you'll move quickly around the room (whether in person or online). To keep the conversation moving, have team members say their name, their department or role, and their answer.

Samples of brief icebreakers:

1. This or That: Ask a simple this-or-that question, such as, "Coffee or tea?" or "Hiking or biking?" Keep the additional chatter to a minimum, but allow people to connect with each other based on their answers.

2. Would You Rather: This is very similar to "This or That" but more action-based. "Would you rather skydive or snow ski?" or

"Would you rather read a book or watch a movie?"

In smaller groups (usually five or less, given the time frame for these gatherings), you can use prompts that take a bit longer to respond to, such as, "Share what attracted you to our company" or "Share a company project or task you've worked on that excites you." Again, have them say their name, department, or role, and then respond to the prompt.

For a full list of icebreakers, visit *The Onboarding Process* Toolbox.

Accessible and Repeatable

Not everyone absorbs information in the same way. When possible, provide the opportunity for the new hire to hear, see, and read information. Send videos or screencasts explaining processes and procedures. Creating a video or screencast can save you time in the long run—you or another team member won't have to relay information to each person individually. Asking your new hire to watch and share something that stood out to them will ensure they've watched it. Ideally, these are housed in a centralized location so they can be referenced at any time employees need them.

As with in-person training, be sure not to overload the new hire with too much information, which may cause them to forget the important content that applies to their daily responsibilities. Spread the information out, when possible, over the ninety-day onboarding process in order of priority.

Welcome Care Package

Consider sending a welcome care package. Some ideas to include would be, but aren't limited to, having breakfast or lunch delivered to their home, a meal delivery gift card (for greater choice), company swag, water bottle, mug, snacks, office supplies (e.g., pens, notepads), or a restaurant gift card for a new-job celebratory dinner with family or friends along with a personalized note.

If you do send a care package, be sure to do it for *all* your new hires, as they will likely share it on social media or among the workplace, and you wouldn't want anyone to feel inferior because they didn't receive a welcome.

Chapter Three

Compliance

The problem with a lot of companies is that HR comes second to their bottom line.

—Gary Vaynerchuk

Compliance can be a scary topic for small business owners. Many feel it is out of their comfort zone, or they don't truly understand what it means. Don't let your fear cause you to bury your head in the sand. Trust us—we've seen some significantly bad situations regarding a lack of compliance in small businesses. Don't put your business, your team, or potentially your personal property and family in jeopardy.

The legalities of labor laws vary from state to state, and data security expectations are constantly evolving. You must invest time and resources to get this part of your business right. Consult with an attorney; be sure you understand all that is legally required to be an employer. It pays to follow the rules, laws, and regulations up front. If not, the damage done to your company may be irreparable.

We don't want to scare you … but we do. Fraud and penalties are real. Set your company up correctly from the start, and make sure each new hire, intern, contractor, and volunteer is properly onboarded in compliance with labor laws.

Paperwork

You will have four types of paperwork for your employees:

1. **Forms** are fillable documents that collect data.

2. **Agreements** require a signature.

3. **Records** consist of forms and signed agreements.

4. **Documents** are informational content.

Consider going paperless with a secure online system that will allow for digital signatures and storage. This is obviously helpful for remote teams, but any company can benefit from handling its paperwork electronically. It allows for quicker completion and easy retrieval. Again, make sure you comply with data protection.

Include a list of all necessary paperwork to be completed on your New Hire Checklist. This checklist will be given to your new hire to help assimilate them during their first ninety days, and it will vary from company to company. An example checklist that you can customize for your business is included in *The Onboarding Process* Toolbox.

Be sure to schedule a meeting with the HR and Finance Departments on the employee's first day. During this meeting, confirm that all paperwork is complete, explain compensation methods, go over benefit options, and answer any questions.

Accounting Department

Much of this paperwork will be federally or state-required forms. These may include I-9, W-4, and other tax forms, possibly required by your state.

Work with your tax and legal professionals to ensure you understand and follow all federal and local labor regulations at all times. You can also refer to the U.S. Department of Labor, dol.gov, for additional information. If outside the United States, be sure to follow the governing regulations in your area.

Other forms may include direct deposit authorization or other items regarding pay or deductions.

HR Department

Your other paperwork will include forms, agreements, and documents that are specific to your company. Some of these need to be written by a legal professional. Consider the type of personnel (volunteers, employees, interns, contractors, transfers) being onboarded and which of the following paperwork would apply:

- Employment agreement
- Non-disclosure agreement (NDA)
- Non-compete agreement
- Non-solicitation agreement
- Independent contractor agreement
- Volunteer waiver
- Other applicable forms for internship

Medical and Emergency Contact Form:

For your employees' safety, it is important to gather relevant medical information that could help during an emergency. This should include contact information for at least two people and any relevant medical details. For example, does your new hire have diabetes or need an epinephrine injector on hand? Ask employees to list any emergency medication they keep with them.

PLEASE NOTE: It is imperative that this information is requested *after* someone is hired and is in no way taken into consideration during the hiring process.

Even in a remote working environment, it is necessary that employees share emergency contact information. What if they were to pass out over a conference call? You can call their local emergency services, but you will need contact information for someone who can report the medical information on their behalf. While this is a rare occurrence, it's better to be prepared. It also shows your team that you care for their health and well-being.

Fun Fact Form:

This information will be helpful for numerous reasons and will allow you to learn more about your new hire. For example, if you are planning a special event, you should know if someone on your team has food allergies or preferences (vegan, gluten-free, etc.). You'll find our Fun Fact Form in *The Onboarding Process* Toolbox.

Here are a some examples of what yours could include:

> *Introduce yourself, elevator-pitch style.*

> *What are you passionate about?*

> *What's your favorite hometown meal?*

If you could visit anywhere in the world, where would you go?

The last book you read was …

Your favorite snack or pick-me-up?

Coffee or tea?

Hobbies or special interests?

Technology or Applicable Department

Depending on your company and the equipment you use, you'll create an Asset List for each employee. Different departments could add to that list, but it will likely start with your Technology Department or possibly HR.

There are three components to this list:

1. Physical technical assets or equipment—may include technology items such as a laptop, phone, or tablet

2. Other physical company assets or equipment, such as a company vehicle, operating equipment, security badge, credit card, etc.

3. Digital assets, such as software and accounts, as well as their unique log-in information to access these assets

You may not want to take the time to create an Asset List as you're busy bringing on a new hire but consider all the assets you'll have to recover should they leave the company. Having everything on one list will keep your assets streamlined and secure.

We recommend reiterating any relevant technology or social media policies here too (more on that later in this chapter). Include a signature line to ensure the new hire reads and understands the parameters of using the company's physical and digital assets. State that software may not be used for any personal reasons. For example, they shouldn't be using company design software for personal use or allowing their child to use their company-issued laptop for online gaming.

When working with outside contractors, they typically provide their own tools (devices, etc.), but there may be

Consider all the assets you'll have to recover should they leave the company.

times you allow them access to a particular software. Be sure to have documentation that shows what they have been allowed access to as well as a proper NDA on file.

A note about sharing software and passwords:

We have seen many small businesses try to take the "easy route" when it comes to software by simply sharing accounts and passwords among multiple team members.

While this may be unavoidable at times, we recommend setting up individual logins for each member utilizing the software when possible. Yes, there may be additional fees for adding more users to certain platforms, but from an asset-security standpoint, it will be worth the cost. If you do have to share an account, list that on the employee's Asset List. The account security would need to be updated upon that employee's exit.

Also, be sure that all employees know not to share passwords, unless it is approved and documented by the Technology Department or Leadership Team. If passwords start floating around a team, shared in one department and then across to another, with no restrictions, you will have completely lost control of any security you had. In that case, when someone exits your company or the team grows, there is no record of who had access to what and if passwords need to be updated. Read more about removing digital access in *The Exit Process.*

Team Handbook

Often with small businesses, the creation of a Team Handbook is either overlooked or thrown together in a hurry as the company rapidly grows. This document is worth the time and effort and is essential to supporting employee retention. When done well, it will benefit both the employee and employer.

A handbook is not a list of what *not* to do. It should be a comprehensive resource regarding all aspects of your company. Use it as an opportunity to share more about your company culture, history, core products, or services. This will assist new hires with learning about your company and be a valuable resource for your entire team—one that can be referred to and accessed openly by all employees, not put on a shelf and forgotten.

Why do you need a Team Handbook?

A Team Handbook

1. Is a communication tool.

2. Clearly sets expectations of professionalism.

3. Explains your company vision, values, and mission.

4. Provides a guide to *company* processes. (Departmental processes can be added but should ideally be given at the departmental level as to not bog down employees who don't need the information.)

5. Assists with compliance. While a handbook isn't required by law, there are specific items that are required to be communicated by the employer to the employee. A Team Handbook is the perfect place to communicate this information. Do your due diligence in compiling the correct information that applies to your company's specific needs.

Tips:

- Your Team Handbook should be a "living" document, reviewed and updated on a regular basis.
- Digital is better than paper. A digital document allows for easier updating and redistributing. Even better, it can be housed in a centralized location for easy access anytime by any team member.
- Include a quick welcome video. This will make the digital handbook more personable.

Continue your team collaboration when crafting your Team Handbook. Review your handbook with key stakeholders. Make sure you have trained professionals weigh in: HR representatives or consultants, as well as employment lawyers, who are up on the latest federal, local, and state laws. It pays to have them review your handbook to ensure that you have not only articulated the information clearly but also that you're not opening yourself up to uncertainty, misinterpretation, or liability. Investing the time now to have your Team Handbook properly vetted will save headaches and resources in the future.

Each business's handbook will look different and may include various elements given the industry and other factors. The following are suggestions of what may be found in a Team Handbook.

Company History and Values

Begin your Team Handbook with an introduction to the company. Include its origin story—when it was founded, by whom, and where. Be careful not make this too lengthy. Just cover the key points that are relevant and will help your team know how to align with your current culture and move toward the company's future goals. This is likely already written and shared on your website.

Next, share about your company culture. Share your Vision Purpose Statement (VPS) and Core Values. But don't simply list them; this is an opportunity to dig in and provide details and definitions. (If you're not familiar with or don't have clarity on your VPS, visit our website, TheJoyOfPursuit.com, for more information.) Include a short story about what inspired the VPS or examples of how the Core Values have been exhibited by employees. This section of the handbook should spark inspiration and excitement about joining the team. All the information you shared about culture during the hiring process should be reiterated here.

Code of Conduct, Policies, and Discipline

This is the section that needs no fluff. It's not as enjoyable, compelling, or inspiring as the previous part of the handbook, but it is vital. Use this section to explain the rules of the company and the non-negotiables. These critical items should be written clearly, concisely, and without excessive use of legal or technical jargon. Ethics and prohibited behaviors need to be stated here. Also, include where the employee can go for resources or support with any situation.

For each rule or policy, outline the consequences of noncompliance. Define the specifics, and don't leave room for something to be misinterpreted. As always, clear communication is essential.

Explain your discipline policy. If you don't have one, now is the time to create it. Most small businesses wish they had one after they need to use it. Your discipline policy guarantees all employees will be treated equally when it comes to disciplinary action. Be proactive and map out a policy that is fair but firm. Some examples would be a "Three Strikes" or "Progressive Discipline" policy.

Define consequences, such as a written warning or probation, and what they entail.

Below are examples of items frequently addressed, but not limited to, in the code of conduct. Some may not be relevant to your company:

- Dress code
- Excessive tardiness
- Meal breaks and rest periods
- Harassment of any kind
- Misuse of company property
- Smoking, alcohol, and substance-abuse guidelines
- Items surrounding legal requirements of the job and violations of (i.e., what happens if an employee's driver's license is revoked when it is a work requirement or if an employee is convicted of a crime that would remove legal clearance to perform job duties)

Include compliance with any governmental laws required by your industry, such as securities, bribery, or conflicts of interest. Again, this is when a professional's recommendations are critical.

Technology, Digital Assets, and Social Media Policy

It's vital to set rules and parameters about what is and isn't allowed in regard to the technology your company provides employees. Your technology policy is one of the main reasons your handbook needs to be reviewed and updated on a regular basis. Be sure your policies are keeping up with and addressing the ever-changing tech world.

Items to address:

- How much privacy is or isn't allowed while utilizing company devices?
- Does the company have the right to view emails that are sent on company devices?

- Are employees allowed to use social media on their work devices? (Think beyond LinkedIn and consider dating apps or other social networking sites.)
- Can an employee connect their personal phone to the company Wi-Fi? If they do, will the same rules apply as when accessing the company network?
- Software and websites should only be accessed for company business, not for personal reasons.
- No sharing passwords, outside *or* inside the company (unless approved by the Technology Department or Leadership Team).

Also, define the consequences of specific offenses regarding technology use, such as pornography, gambling, illegal activity, or hate speech.

A special note regarding social media for personal and business use: If your company utilizes social media platforms to conduct business and interact with clients, you need to clearly define what is and is not expected of your employees.

For example, say you hire someone to moderate and answer client questions in a group on a social media platform. The employee needs to know that they are expected to use a social media profile for this function, but they do not have to use their personal account. Your company may have standards for said profile, such as a professional headshot, place of employment, etc. However, a company cannot dictate that someone do the same for their personal profile. The employee must always have the option to keep their personal profile separate and to set up a professional profile (meeting the company requirements) to use when working on behalf of the company.

Furthermore, explain to employees that they do not have to accept "follow," "friend," or private message requests from clients on their personal profiles and accounts. There needs to be a clear line between what is personal and what is business related. Allow and support your employees with this boundary. You may even provide a polite but professional message they can share in response to client requests, directing the requester to the proper resource.

Equal Opportunity Employment and Non-Discrimination Policy

Many businesses are required by the U.S. Department of Labor to share that they offer equal opportunity employment and do not allow for discrimination in the workplace.

As a leader, it is your responsibility to set the tone and expectations when it comes to equality and respect. Employees must know that discrimination or harassment of any kind will not be tolerated in the workplace. Even if you think this should go without saying, you should still say it.

Provide resources for how to report incidences. We recommend consulting with your attorney regarding what legal demands your company must follow. If your business is in the United States, you can view more details here: <u>dol.gov</u>. If you are outside the U.S., please check with your governing authorities.

Compensation and Benefits

Compensation and benefit details should have been discussed (and possibly negotiated) during the hiring process and provided in writing with the job offer. Reiterate all general details again in your handbook.

The compensation section will include details about the following:

- What hours (minimum or maximum) are required of part-time and full-time employees

- What is considered overtime and the overtime pay rate
- What federal- or state-required payroll deductions will come out of their paycheck (social security, medicare, federal and state withholding taxes)
- Pay schedule (weekly, bimonthly, or monthly)
- Commission or bonus opportunities and rates
- How to clock or track hours for employees paid on an hourly basis

Benefit options will vary greatly from company to company. The most common include:

- Insurance (health, dental, vision, life, disability, etc.)
- Stock options
- 401(k) plans (and employer matching, if applicable)

- Car allowance or other financial allowances

Note: If a sign-on bonus is promised, but it's not standard company policy, you will not include that information in your handbook. Just be sure the details of the bonus were included in the new hire's official job offer. Don't neglect to specify if there is a waiting period before the bonus is paid.

The above details can be complicated. Communicate them as clearly as possible. Include information about enrollment periods and who to contact for support.

Your company may also provide nontraditional benefits to your employees. Share the details of these here, including the process of how to activate or redeem these benefits.

Nontraditional benefits can provide an incredible amount of value to your employees and be an extension of your company culture.

If you don't offer any benefits, you may want to consider some. Not only do employee benefits provide a competitive advantage during recruitment, but they also benefit the company by creating happy and loyal employees.

Some nontraditional benefits could include:

- Tuition reimbursement or assistance
- Discounted services or products
- Wellness memberships
- Housekeeping services
- Counseling and mental health resources
- Nutritional counseling
- Childcare assistance
- Shared library
- Professional development (company organized or costs covered for external opportunities)
- Memberships to clubs or organizations that fit the company culture

- Family discounts or other memberships

When discussing benefits, also address any conditions or limitations. Is there a waiting period before all benefits can be accessed?

Workers' Compensation Policy

A workers' compensation insurance policy protects your employees by providing them financial compensation if they are injured on the job. The technicalities, requirements, and legalities of this are different depending on your state and the size of the business. We recommend this be at the top of your list to discuss with a professional and be sure to clearly communicate the details of this policy in your handbook.

Time Off: Vacation and Leave

It is best practice to provide the same amount of time off for every employee of the same status (part time versus full time). Once someone has worked for your company for a certain amount of time, an increase in time off is commonly given. Of course, there may be exceptions to your policy, especially with the C-Suite or Leadership Team. If you do offer an employee beyond what is listed in your handbook, be sure to do so in writing.

There could be several components to your vacation and leave policy. Here we will touch on some specifics you need to provide.

Paid or unpaid vacation

- Does this increase with years of service to the company?
- Are the vacation days accrued monthly or granted after a specific length of employment?
- What is the process for scheduling time off and requesting approval, and how much notice is required?

Sick or medical leave

- Who should the employee contact if sick and via what method?
- Is a doctor's note required if work is missed for a certain number of days?
- Some states require a specific number of sick days be given to employees. Be sure your policies are in compliance.

Maternity/paternity/adoption leave

- Many companies choose to offer beyond what is legally required.
- This could include paid time off or an extended time frame when compared to regular medical leave.

Paid family leave

- Some companies offer this to support parents or caregivers. It can go a long way in showing your employees that you care for them and their families.

Legally mandated leave

- The Family Medical Leave Act (FMLA) is enforced by the U.S. Department of Labor. Standards may vary for certain labor laws depending on your state.
- Other leave-of-absence policies are required by law in addition to FMLA. These could include jury duty, military leave, and time off to vote; therefore, they may be required to be communicated to your employees.

Holidays

- What holidays are observed?
- Are the holidays paid time off?
- If these holidays are worked, are they paid at an additional (higher) holiday pay rate?

Separation and Termination Policy

This section of your handbook is one you don't want to have to use, but it is vital to share with all employees. Work with your legal expert to clearly define what should or shouldn't be included.

Some questions to think through include the following:

- What steps does an employee need to take if they want to resign?
- Is a written notice required, or can they submit their resignation verbally?
- Should this be taken to the HR Department or their direct supervisor?
- Is a two-week notice requested?
- What is the employee entitled to if they are terminated and for how long (such as medical insurance coverage or any of the additional bonuses previously mentioned)?

Confidentiality Policy

To prevent the misuse of confidential information, it is essential to define what exactly is considered confidential. Your company is bound by law to protect certain information. List such details in your handbook to make your employees aware of what can and cannot be shared. Among other things, this will likely include your company's internal business plan, your clients' information, including but not limited to their emails and credit cards on file, and employees' financial accounts or personal information. Again, when including any policy, lay out the consequences of not adhering to the policy.

Workplace Safety

Set up policies and procedures to protect the safety of your entire team while on the job. Not only is it ethical to ensure workplace safety, but it's also required by law. The Occupational Safety and Health Act

(OSHA) requires you to provide a working environment free from recognized hazards that cause, or could potentially cause, death or physical harm to your employees. Your Team Handbook should describe in detail what you will do to prevent injury and illness, as well as what your employees are required to do, such as reporting accidents or potential safety hazards and complying with all applicable safety policies. Visit osha.gov for the most up-to-date information. If outside the U.S., be sure to check with your governing authorities specifically for safety concerns in the workplace.

Remote Work Policy

If your employees work remotely or have the option of a hybrid work schedule, clearly define any requirements. Some of these could include the following:

- When to be "logged on" and available
- Expectations of response time
- Check-ins or status updates

- Meeting attendance requirements

Note: Employers sometimes confuse employee and contractor status when a company is working remotely. Be sure you aren't expecting employee-level responsibility from an independent contractor.

Other Possible Policies

Depending on your company and advice from your attorney, you may need to include other policies. Here are some frequently suggested items:

- Company vehicle use
- Company credit card use or expense reports
- Networking and entertaining—When is it allowed or appropriate to entertain a client, and what parameters are set?

- Parameters regarding family members working within the same company and department
- Restrictions on dating or romantic relationships (typically defined as prohibited between supervisors and subordinates)
- When gifts from customers or vendors (in any form) can be accepted (Or are they considered bribes?)
- If employees are allowed to accept tips from customers
- Document management
- Media and press communication
- Uniforms

Performance Reviews

Employees want to be recognized and desire your feedback. Your company needs a defined process for handling performance reviews for all employees. This element slips through the cracks in many small businesses; don't let yours be one of them.

At a minimum, provide a brief overview of the process in your Team Handbook. Include how frequently employees are reviewed, who conducts the review, and other necessary details of the process.

Refer to *The Retention Process* for more guidance and tools to set up a performance review process that will strengthen and protect this most valuable asset—your team.

Employee Acknowledgment

Yes, your new hire needs to sign off, indicating that they have received, read, and understood the Team Handbook. This is critical should you encounter any future issues with disciplinary action, for instance, a wrongful termination lawsuit—that signature will support your defense. Consult with your attorney about what to include. Here is a sample of specific language in the agreement:

> *The handbook is not a binding contract and does not guarantee further employment. The handbook is the final word on all policies, superseding any memos or documents that may have been circulated to employees before its inception. Policies are subject to change, and this document will be updated to reflect those changes in a timely manner.*

You have the right to change policies as your business shifts and evolves; however, you also must disclose any pertinent updates that would affect your employees. Your handbook should be reviewed annually to make sure it is still accurate. If updates are required, make those in a timely manner and redistribute to employees to sign. If your handbook is digital, updating will be simple, and your team can digitally sign off once they've reviewed the updates.

The above suggestions are simply that—suggestions. It's imperative that you review state and federal laws when writing certain policies. We also recommend the guidance of a lawyer who is familiar with your state labor laws.

Chapter Four

Clarification

The only thing worse than training your employees and having them leave is not training them and having them stay.

—Henry Ford

Setting your new hire up for success means making sure they are clear on expectations, processes, job duties, start times, and so on. Clarity breeds confidence. Providing a clear-cut schedule and understandable goals from the start will allow your new hire to confidently step into their new role.

Onboarding Schedule

First-Day Schedule

The Hiring Manager should work with other key team players to create a schedule for your new hire's first day. Share this schedule with all involved during early onboarding (the time between the job offer and their first day). Make the first day memorable—in a good way. Put your new hire at ease by letting them know where they are going and when.

Welcome them at the door or show up early online if meeting via video conference. If you are a hybrid company, make sure they know if they will be meeting in person or online on their first day. If possible, give a welcome gift when the new hire arrives (company swag, office supplies, apparel, etc.) to let them know you're happy they're here.

Be structured and organized with your onboarding schedule. As mentioned in Chapter 2, avoid providing too much at once or pointing your new hire in a million directions. Allow them time to process and finish before moving on to the next thing. Keep a list of anything you think of throughout the day that didn't make it into the schedule. Add these in during extra time or restructure the week's schedule to include them.

Here are the top items to include in the first-day schedule:

- Gather for a welcome meeting at the start of the day.
- Set up workspace (if applicable).
- Meet with HR and/or Finance to ensure all required paperwork is complete and the new hire's questions are answered.
- Connect the new hire with their mentor (see more on this in Chapter 5).
- Allow time for the new hire to get to know others on the team. Schedule a team lunch, even if virtual. Do not discuss work during this time. The priority is to

build relationships. Refer to Chapter 2 for icebreaker questions.

* Dedicate time for orientation (details provided in Chapter 5).
* Provide specific job/tasks training.
* Debrief at the end of the day.

Allow quiet time for the new hire to read and review materials, but don't make their onboarding a solo experience. Never silo a new hire or have only one person onboarding them. Remember, building relationships will increase retention.

First-Day Schedule Example

8:00 - 8:15 a.m.	Welcome with HR manager
8:15 - 8:40 a.m.	Tour
8:45 - 9:15 a.m.	Set up workspace and technology
9:15 - 10:15 a.m.	Finalize paperwork and benefit set up
10:30 - 11:45 a.m.	Meet with supervisor
11:45 - 12:45 p.m.	Team lunch
1:00 - 2:00 p.m.	Meet mentor
2:00 - 3:30 p.m.	Orientation
3:30 - 4:00 p.m.	Buffer time to catch up revisit workspace
4:00 - 5:00 p.m.	End of day debrief

Notes

_____
_____
_____
_____
_____

First-Week Schedule

Create a New Hire Checklist and include tasks the new employee needs to accomplish within their first week. Don't throw them into the deep end, though. These tasks include paperwork, email passwords, and other basics. We'll cover goal-setting later in this chapter.

During this first week, continue to schedule bookend meetings at the beginning and end of each day with the direct supervisor. This is an opportunity to check in, address concerns, and continue to put your new hire at ease.

As the week progresses, the new hire will spend less time on orientation and more time on job-specific training. Be sure to allow for some buffer time to get caught up. You don't want to rush your new hire from one thing to another or not get the necessities completed in a timely manner.

Put time limits or expectations on independent reading, studying, and training. It should never take a new hire a full forty-hour week to read the orientation material, watch videos, and so on. Allow time to review the Team Handbook and other information but mix in other activities so your new hire isn't stuck in a cubicle or in front of their computer all day watching or reading training information.

Combining hands-on training and face-to-face introductions, without moving too quickly from one to the other, will provide a fresh and energetic feeling to onboarding without causing confusion, chaos, or pure boredom.

New Hire Checklist

☐ Review Team Handbook

Paperwork to complete:

- ☐ I-9
- ☐ W-4
- ☐ Direct deposit
- ☐ Employment agreement
- ☐ Non-disclosure agreement (NDA)
- ☐ Non-compete agreement
- ☐ Non-solicitation agreement
- ☐ Medical and Emergency Contact Form
- ☐ Fun Fact Form
- ☐ Review and sign off on Asset List
- ☐ Acknowledgment of Team Handbook

Meet with:

- ☐ Hiring Manager to review paperwork and onboarding schedule.
- ☐ Mentor and establish meeting schedule.
- ☐ Key players in other departments.

☐ Introduction meeting with team.

☐ Complete orientation modules.

☐ Complete Onboarding Feedback Form.

Training

There are two sides to training in the onboarding process. The first is overall company systems training, which could be managed by videos or group sessions. Don't neglect to provide training for these systems. While many of them may seem easy or you may think, "Everyone probably knows that," never make assumptions. If there is a tool that must be used a certain way, provide clear instructions to do so. Remember, things that come easy to you or to some may not to others. It is better to provide the training than to assume.

For small businesses wanting to streamline their training, create a "how-to" video library. If your HR Department doesn't include someone who is comfortable or personable on camera, you can outsource this. A video library's usefulness will extend beyond a new hire's training. Other employees can access the library when they come to a roadblock or forget how to do something.

A video library serves three purposes:

1. It provides an example of the correct way to do something, creating a standard for all employees in the company.

2. It allows employees to troubleshoot and resolve issues on their own without needing to ask for help from their supervisor, colleague, or the Technology Department, which will save time and resources.

3. It frees you from repetitive training when onboarding multiple employees.

Here are some suggestions of how-to videos that may be beneficial to a small business:

- Setting up or updating an email signature to a company standard
- Setting up an email auto-response when out of the office

- Standards for how to name and where to save electronic files
- How to file a completed expense report
- Where to find company reference documents (Team Directory or Handbook)
- Communication platform etiquette (e.g., how to only notify relevant members and not the entire team)
- Tips for using software or programs more efficiently
- How to protect your computer and clear your cache
- How to troubleshoot a common software error (This is the opportunity for your Technology Department to consider the most common issues/queries they handle, then create a video about how employees can fix the problem themselves, if applicable.)

Gather a list of your most frequently asked company-wide questions. Then, if easier to show than tell, make videos that answer those questions. If you can simply create an FAQ sheet, include this in your Team Handbook.

The second type of training is role specific. This is where the department supervisor will take the lead on providing or delegating training. If delegated, be sure the trainer is up to date and follows procedures properly. The last thing you want is to train someone in someone else's bad habits.

Make the effort to train correctly. Habits are hard to break. Be sure the new team member is trained well and not learning things the wrong way. This means that you may need the department supervisor to spend valuable time working with the new hire. You may think their time is best spent elsewhere and be tempted to designate another employee to do the training. But if that employee doesn't train the new hire well, the supervisor will end up spending more time correcting errors and behavior in the long run. This does not bode well for the new hire or the supervisor.

The first step is to identify what training the employee needs. Refer back to the Job Description you used during their hiring process. What tools, systems, documents, processes, and procedures do they need to know? Also, look back at the new hire's Screening Questions and Skills Assessment (see Chapter 4 of *The Hiring Process*). Were there particular tools they had experience with or some they don't know at all? Customize the training experience to fit the new hire's personal skill level.

Suggestions for training topics:

- Processes and procedures
- Paper or electronic filing structures
- Products and services (be sure to include costs and deliverables)
- Software, tools, and equipment, including applications used for interoffice communication

Shadowing is a great way for a new hire to experience a procedure or tool without slowing down the process or pulling a trainer away from day-to-day responsibilities. Make sure you set limits on what and for how long a new hire is shadowing, as you are now paying two people to accomplish one task. Still, shadowing (hands-on) is better than pulling a trainer from a project to sit and talk about it instead of accomplishing it.

One topic we can't stress enough and that is often overlooked during training is communication.

If your new hire doesn't know the structure of company

Good communication is essential to a healthy team.

communication, you cannot provide clarity for their role and responsibilities. Good communication is essential to a successful business and a healthy team. Your Leadership Team should take the time to define expectations for communication in your company. Each department should specify the best practices for them. Don't neglect cascading messages or rippling information—how does information get from one department to another or to the entire company?

Many businesses use multiple types of software, platforms, or systems that can serve as communication tools. Part of this training is about how to communicate effectively and efficiently. The other part is about etiquette.

Regarding etiquette, does your company expect meetings to be free of distractions? If so, train your new hire on this standard. Make a clear statement that all notifications should be muted during meetings.

While communication platforms can be efficient, there needs to be a clear understanding of how each should be used in order to maintain efficiency. For example, if your company uses both email and internal communication platforms, what practices are followed for emailing within the company? Should email only be utilized when including those outside of the company (i.e., vendors or clients)? This rule will likely keep team communication more efficient on the internal software.

Multiple options for communication are especially common in virtual and hybrid work settings.

But don't forget about communication etiquette for when everyone works in the same building. Is

Communication etiquette is essential for productivity.

it appropriate to just walk into someone's office when you have a question? Should a request for a meeting be sent? Keep efficiency, practicality, and clarity in mind when considering communication methods. If communication is an ongoing issue for your company, we discuss in depth specific types of communication for businesses in *The Retention Process*.

Here is an example as to why training on communication practices is so important.

We once worked with a small business that purchased a communication platform for their team. It was greatly needed to improve team communication. However, the leadership didn't take the time to define and share best practices with their team. This platform had the ability to post content that would distribute to every person in the company and individually notify them. One team member repeatedly would ask questions on the platform that should have been directed to a single person rather than the entire company. She would ask a question on the platform that should have been directed to a single person rather than the entire company. We equate her poor etiquette to a school building where someone continually uses the loudspeaker to broadcast their questions to every classroom instead of contacting a specific teacher.

This behavior caused several problems:

1. It created a company-wide distraction. Think about the time lost when this happened on a regular basis.
2. The team member with the answer would reply on the same inappropriate platform. Thus, the company-wide distraction continued.
3. These distractions led to frustration among team members. Those who better understood how to use the platform would complain to others, "Why doesn't she just ask one person her questions?" Hence more distractions and lost time.
4. This bad habit was then replicated by other team members and new hires. "I see that she asks all of her questions here. I guess that's what I'm supposed to do too."
5. When too many distractions like this occur, it becomes noise, and your team

will be conditioned to tune out valuable information.

6. Letting this get out of hand is horrible for company culture as it appears no one is in charge and correcting this poor behavior.

Solution: Address such situations quickly. Privately let the offender know the appropriate way to use the software. This may include walking her through the proper steps or directing her to a training video. Remove the content from the wrong place so others don't feel obligated to respond and thereby put an end to the distractions.

Another issue with multiple internal communication platforms is when team members don't understand which one to use. Perhaps they send the same message across all platforms and disrupt the workflow multiple times. The result is confusion about where to send the answer. This is especially harmful if done by your Leadership Team.

They can open the door for bad habits to spread. As they lead, others will follow.

While one incident may seem insignificant, if continued, it has a snowball effect that leads to more wasted time and lack of efficiency. This can have a negative impact on your company's culture. Culture affects your productivity. Productivity affects your bottom line. Little things matter. Onboarding matters.

Setting Goals

All employees want to feel valued. Keep this in mind during onboarding when establishing goals and expectations. Help the new hire understand how their talents and strengths complement the department or company. If they can see how their day-to-day responsibilities contribute to the overall success of the company, they will have a better understanding of how valuable they are. This is especially important for entry-level positions, frontline workers, behind-the-scenes employees, and service workers.

For example, the hotel housekeeper knows the cost of a room per night is $179. If a guest complains about the cleanliness of the room and wants a refund, the company loses more than $179. They lose the revenue, not to mention the marketing dollars spent to bring that guest to the hotel in the first place, and they also take a hit to their reputation, especially if the guest vents about the situation on social media. The hotel housekeeper needs to understand the whole picture, not just the per-room cost.

Every position matters—otherwise we wouldn't need to fill it. Make sure your new hire understands their value in big-picture terms.

Speaking of, when setting goals for your new hire, start with the big picture in mind. Clarify what your company goals are and their timelines. From there, share departmental goals. Explain what metrics, reporting, and other details go into measuring goal success. Also, share what methods are used to hold each other accountable for goal completion.

When a new employee can imagine their exciting future at your company, they will be more likely to work hard and stay long term, which supports the company goals. Having your new hire heading in the right direction from day one is important so as to not derail the rest of the team.

Once the big picture is clearly painted, focus on establishing goals for the new hire. Success can only be achieved if the goal is communicated with clarity. Refer to the Job Description that was used during their hiring. What problem was originally defined when creating that Job Description? They need to understand their purpose and how that supports the company VPS. Explain how their individual goals support the team goals as well as the overall company goals.

We recommend that the onboarding process lasts ninety days, but you can tailor it to fit your company's needs. With this schedule in mind, start at the ninety-day mark and work backward to set certain milestones. Use our Goal MAP to guide you through this process. See the example below. You can also access a blank worksheet in *The Onboarding Process Toolbox*.

Goal MAP

Goal State in one sentence or word that will be easily recognized on the calendar by all involved in the completion of it.

Due Date
6/30

Create and roll-out company-wide Team Calendar

What problem does it solve? Frequent confusion regarding the timing and location of important meetings. Absenteeism and tardiness. Overbooked calendars. Questions about company holidays.

What solution does it provide? Accurate information in a centralized location.

Coordinates How is this moving you in the direction of the company Vision?
The calendar will assist with important company-wide information being communicated.

Measurable (quantity, results, deadline)

Team Calendar created, including all company holidays and meetings and shared to team by June 30.

Accomplished with
(supplies, software, tools OR people via delegation, coordination, or input)

G-suite calendar
Integrator
HR
Tech

Process to completion	Due Dates
Break your goal into milestones	
Step 1 Confirm holidays & meetings with HR	4/15
Step 2 Input all dates, times, and locations into calendar.	4/28
Step 3 Coordinate with tech to ensure everyone has access.	5/10
Step 4 Create "how-to access" screencast & FAQ doc.	5/22
Step 5 Develop rollout plan with Integrator.	6/1
Final Review Submit for Leadership team review and approval.	6/15
Describe what complete looks like	
"How-to access" screencast & FAQs shared with the team.	
Team Calendar is in use & accessible by all employees.	

Add milestone dates to your calendar and anyone else's working with you on this goal.

What does success look like in three months for the new hire? What will they accomplish in that time frame? Are they fully trained and working independently? What will they create, implement, or sell during that time?

Once the ninety-day goal(s) is (are) set, work with the new hire to divide them into actionable steps and milestones. To reach this goal within ninety days, what needs to be completed by day thirty? Day sixty? Keep this time frame realistic to the learning curve your new hire is facing.

Also, drill down to smaller, short-term goals (i.e., daily and weekly goals) and add these to their calendars. These short-term goals will allow your new hire to soon feel involved in the company operations. While you don't want to overwhelm them, you do want to give them something to own. This should be something manageable that allows them to feel accomplished and recognize their value.

Small goals for the first week could be the onboarding items your new hire completes individually, such as "Review Modules 1–3 of systems training." No matter how small the achievement, the point is to calendar their goals for the first ninety days.

Let the new hire know what to expect in regard to accountability and feedback on their goals. Will their supervisor ask for a weekly progress report? Do all team members share a status update in monthly meetings? Their supervisor should work closely with them, providing constructive feedback and making sure they have all the direction and tools needed to be successful.

Chapter Five

Connection

The real competitive advantage in any business is one word only, which is people.

—Kamil Toume

The focus of this chapter is two-fold:

1. We will review resources that connect your new hire with fellow team members,
2. and we will discuss how to connect your new hire to the appropriate tools.

People spend a significant portion of their lives at work. Forming strong and meaningful bonds with coworkers is critical for effective teamwork, job satisfaction, and employment retention. Connecting with other team members also imparts the basic understanding of who does what in the organization so your team knows who to go to or direct others to.

Team Directory

Provide new hires with a Team Directory. This will put faces with names, help them learn everyone's roles, and enable them to contact others in the company.

Don't have a Team Directory? Now is the time to create one.

Your Team Directory should include a headshot, name, department, email, and work phone number (or extension). As mentioned before, digital is always better. It is much easier to update and distribute, and it can be better protected, keeping your important team information safe from spammers and headhunters. This directory should be easily accessible to all team members at all times. It may be part of your existing interoffice communication software. If so, provide instruction on how to access it.

Team Directory Example

Amanda Painter
Cofounder & CFO
Extension 123
email@company
Birthday: June 9
Joined team 2021

Brenda Haire
Cofounder & CEO
Extension 124
email@company
Birthday: January 26
Joined team 2021

For more personalization and to build more connection, you may include:

- When the person started with the company
- Birthdate (month and day *only*)

Important: Do not include employees' private information in your Team Directory (or via any other method). This could include, but is not limited to, the following:

- Personal phone number
- Home address
- Age
- Information about children or spouse

Organization, Accountability, and Responsibility (OAR) Chart

When done well, an OAR Chart provides important information that can be used as an onboarding tool. But don't just hand your OAR Chart to the new hire. Discuss it and show them how to use it. Help them learn the hierarchy and how information flows up, down, and across departments.

Understanding how departments are organized, who holds others accountable, what each person is responsible for, the company chain of command, and how the organization is connected benefits all employees, but it is especially helpful to a new hire who is trying to learn the lay of the land.

When this tool is used correctly, you should never hear someone say, "Oh, John at the end of the hall? I have no idea what he does." John's entry on the chart will clearly show what department he works in, what level of accountability he holds, and what his top responsibilities are.

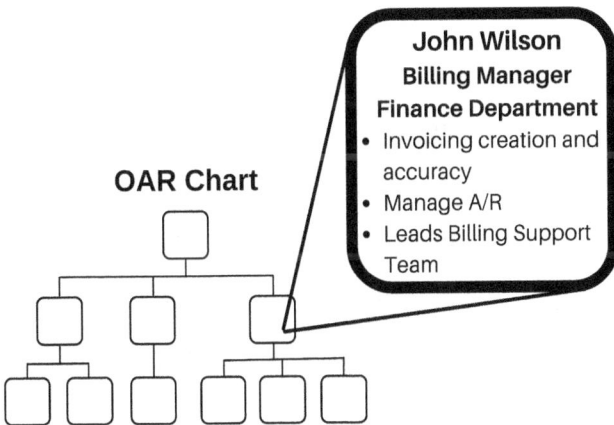

OAR Chart

John Wilson
Billing Manager
Finance Department
- Invoicing creation and accuracy
- Manage A/R
- Leads Billing Support Team

The same holds true for an OAR Chart as for the Team Directory when it comes to keeping it current and openly accessible to all employees at any time. And again, this is for internal use only and shouldn't be distributed publicly.

If you decide to include any team information on your website, make sure to get permission from the team member about what you may include and which, if any, photograph will accompany the information.

Setup and Access

Connection reaches beyond the people in a company. Connecting your new hire includes providing them access to all organizational tools and software needed to do their job well. Much of this work will involve your Technology Department. Have them provide or assist the new hire with password setup, if necessary. Offer a quick tutorial (or video link) for each tool to ensure access.

This needs to be scheduled in advance for two reasons:

1. Your new hire will likely need to access these tools while in training.

2. The Tech Team needs to be ready and available to help early in the process.

Here are some items your new hire will likely need to be connected to:

- Email—If possible, set this up (including their e-signature) prior to their first day.
- Communication platforms—Think through all the groups and channels the new hire needs to join and what information they will need to access in those groups and channels.
- Software and program access—These may include project/task management tools, your Client Relationship Management (CRM) system, etc.
- Documents—Allow access to to-do lists, goals, or other planning documents to set the new hire up for a great start.

- Company calendar—Invite to all events, calendars, regularly scheduled meetings, et cetera, making sure important dates are booked with plenty of notice.

Tip: Create guidelines for how to best utilize the calendar to manage connections, such as inviting people to events, providing any necessary links or agendas in the notes, and setting their online meeting software to automatically connect, if applicable.

Stay Connected with Regular Check-Ins

Hiring Managers should stay available and accessible during the new hire's onboarding season, but they should also avoid micromanaging. Regular check-ins as needed with their new hires, including the new hire's supervisor, should do the trick. These can decrease in frequency as the new hire gets acclimated to the job but don't neglect them. Stay engaged.

During the first week, the direct supervisor will connect with them at least twice a day, if not more. After that, the frequency can decrease to daily, then weekly, and eventually monthly, ending with an Onboarding Review at the end of the first ninety days.

During these check-ins:

- Review checklists.
- Evaluate progress on goals.
- Answer questions.
- Ensure they have the resources they need to get their job done.
- Give feedback (good or bad) on job performance. (Keep it constructive.)
- Ask for feedback on how they are adjusting and how the process is working for them.

The direct supervisor should then relay information from these updates to the Hiring Manager and/or the Leadership Team—however information flows within your company.

You'll conduct a final Onboarding Review and ask for feedback before this process is complete. We will discuss this review in depth in Chapter 7. At any point during these check-ins, you can let your new hire know the frequency of future check-ins and about the upcoming Onboarding Review. Keeping those lines of communication open are important.

Chapter Six

Culture

Corporate culture is the only sustainable competitive advantage that is completely within the control of the entrepreneur. Develop a strong corporate culture first and foremost.

—David Cummings

Orientation

Company orientation is an important component of the onboarding process. This part of onboarding should be the same for all new hires, regardless of their position. The goal of orientation is not to train on job specifics but to immerse the new hire in the culture of your company and provide additional information regarding company policies.

During orientation, the Hiring Manager will spend time reviewing any specific handbook information that needs to be discussed and answering any questions regarding company policies.

The orientation process should also include company leadership (i.e., your C-Suite or Executive Team). Have the owner or a Leadership Team member spend one-on-one time with the new hire to discuss the mission and values of the company, preferably someone who helped craft these elements.

There is no one better to relay the vision of the company to a new hire. Don't beat a dead horse

The goal of orientation is to immerse the new hire in your culture.

if this was a deep topic during your hiring process, but remember that the more you talk about these key culture items, the more they will understand their importance.

This Leadership Team member should also share information about the company's current strategic plan. Who is your target market? Who do you serve? Tie in how the new hire contributes to the overall mission.

Provide a general overview of your products and services. If the new hire doesn't understand how money is made, how will they understand the part they play in the flow of cash, both in and out of the company?

Be sure to provide a list or glossary of acronyms or unique terms used by the company. This could be included in your Team Handbook or supplemental documentation.

Tip: Consider required reading, depending on your company and the position. Are there principles from a team-building book your company specifically implements?

Keep in mind that orientation doesn't have to be completed all on the first day. Depending on your team size and the amount of information to share, you may spread orientation throughout the ninety days.

Mentoring

We highly recommend providing a mentor for all new hires in your company. And yes, we have heard all the excuses for why some companies don't want to do this. The top excuse is that the mentor will spend time away from their normal job duties, and there is a cost associated with that. But trust us—it is worth it. Investing in your team will produce the biggest return.

First, it's important to understand the role of a mentor.

A mentor is

- A guide to company culture.

- Naturally compassionate in the workplace.
- An example of your company's Core Values.
- Clear regarding your company's mission and can articulate it.
- A facilitator of relationships and team-building.
- More experienced within the company or role.
- Available to provide support and answer questions.
- Looking out for the best interest of the company and the new hire.

A mentor is not

- A trainer or coach.
- A mediator between the mentee and their supervisor.
- Their direct supervisor (if company size allows).
- Boastful or a gossip.

- Using the title to gain financially or otherwise.
- On company probation or in violation of any company policies.

The goal of providing a mentor for your new hire is to further instill your company culture in them. Mentorship shows both the mentor and the new hire that they are valued and that the company cares about their growth and development. It makes a statement that they are worth the extra time to be mentored. Overall, mentorship will add tremendous value to the new hire, to the mentor, and in return, to your company.

The mentor's focus is not to train the new hire on processes. Rather, it is to provide an example of company culture as one who has the capacity and interpersonal skills to listen and support the new hire. Mentors guide them through learning the ins and outs of the company. The mentor does not need to be in

HR or even the same department as your new team member. The mentor is not responsible for overseeing the onboarding process; they are only a component of it.

A word of caution, though: the mentor must be a shining star on your team. This is crucial. The mentor must embody your company's Core Values and be a leading example of individual performance balanced with teamwork. The mentor understands policies and procedures, strives for excellence, and is dedicated to company goals.

Don't force mentorship on someone who does not meet these criteria. It will create more harm than good. A mentor

The mentor should exemplify your Core Values.

should be in a position of tenure or a position your new hire would strive to achieve. Never pair two new hires. On the flip side, don't choose the person who has been at your company the longest just because they should know the most about your company. Being a mentor is a skill, a privilege, and a gift.

Connect your new hire with their mentor on their first day of work and have them establish a regular meeting schedule. Also, be sure to include clear parameters in this working relationship. What method of communication is preferred? Should all questions be saved until the next scheduled meeting? Take the time to clearly communicate to the mentee what role their mentor does and does not serve. The mentor/mentee relationship should continue through at least the first quarter, if not longer, but it is important to include the timeline from the start to help both the mentor and new hire understand the expectations. Provide your mentor with a checklist of items to cover with their mentee. You can view our suggestions for the Mentor Checklist in *The Onboarding Process* Toolbox.

Mentors are useful if your company culture is healthy. If your company culture isn't what you'd like it to be or you're not really sure what it is, the third book in this series, *The Retention Process: Create a Culture of Worth in the Workplace*, will help. In it, we discuss in depth how to create a culture that teams won't want to leave and candidates will flock to.

Chapter Seven

Wrap-up and Resources

No company, small or large, can win over the long run without energized employees who believe in the mission and understand how to achieve it.

—Jack Welch

Congratulations! You are nearing the end of your onboarding process. The onboarding period will officially end with an Onboarding Review. The goal is to assess the new hire's progress during their first ninety days:

1. Identify any additional training needs.
2. Evaluate their performance.
3. Ensure all orientation items are complete.

Use the Onboarding ScoreCARD included in the Toolbox. Be sure not to neglect the review, as it signifies the end of the onboarding process for both your team and the new hire. Here is an example of a ScoreCARD. This is to be completed by the supervisor and then reviewed with the new hire.

Onboarding ScoreCARD

Employee Name Brad Robbins _____ **Hire Date** _3/28/22_____

Supervisor conducting review
Carol Burns _____ **Review Date** _7/6/22_____

Are all orientation items complete? (YES) NO
Review Goal MAP. Have goals been met? (YES) NO
If no to either - identify the source of the problem and what corrective steps need to be taken._____
  N/A

Rate on a 1-10 scale (in the box provided).
Provide a specific example (positive or negative) for each.

[10] **C**ulture –does the employee exhibit the Core Values?
  Brad has shown his desire to be a lifelong learner by diving
  into tools and systems he is unfamiliar with.

[8] **A**bility–has the employee shown the ability to complete the job
  duties? Any gaps in knowledge or skill?
  Yes, he has shown competency with all Google WS tools needed for
  his role. Especially the calendar. He had some questions regarding
  Excel but has been resourceful to find the answers he needs.

[9] **R**ole–has the employee shown an understanding of their role,
  responsibilities, and where they fit into the overall company picture?
  Brad has stepped right in with his role as Strategic Assistant.
  Specifically with anticipating my needs prior to meetings by
  providing locations and agendas.

[10] **D**esire–does the employee show a desire to continue in this role
  and to continue working for the company?
  Absolutely! Brad has taken the initiative to plan improvements for
  the next company-wide meeting. Showing his commitment and
  enthusiasm in how he supports the overall mission.

Additional training needs
Brad is ready to tackle learning our CRM system. Tech will
provide access to training modules and time for hands-on
learning.

Strategies for improvement or growth
He shows interest and the ability to facilitate the weekly
admin meetings. This will provide growth in his position. Susan
will work with him to understand the agenda and components
of the meeting. We'll include this in his Goal MAP for next Q.

At the end of the onboarding period, the new hire should also have the opportunity to evaluate your company's onboarding process. Requesting feedback from new hires shows that you value their insights and will assist you with keeping your onboarding process successful. Make sure that the new team member understands that this information will be confidential and only shared with the individuals who can better the process.

You can find a blank Onboarding Feedback Form in the Toolbox. Here is a completed sample that shows how this tool can collect valuable insight for your company about your onboarding process.

Onboarding Feedback Form

Rate each of these items. (10 = no improvement needed)

9 Orientation program

8 Mentor program

8 Training for your specific role

9 Overall Onboarding Process

Give examples of when you have seen our Core Values in action _Susan has shared stories with me of her life-long_ _learning with the company and supported me with mine by_ _providing resources and coaching_

Tim owns his accountability well by admitting mistakes and _taking responsibility for errors. But by then taking measures_ _to correct the issue and avoid it in the future._

How would you describe the last 3 months?
Fantastic! I am enjoying my time here. I see room for _growth and development._

What was the most (and least) helpful part of the onboarding process? _The Orientation time spent with the_ _individual members of the leadership team provided so much_ _value and insight into the company culture and history. It_ _also showed that I am valued being a member of this team._

What suggestions would you make to strengthen it?
I think the mentor program is great, but it could be _stronger in regards to prompts for discussion topics._

Which co-worker(s) have been most helpful since you arrived? _Carol. She's been patient with teaching me and showing_ _me the ropes. She's made a point to set me up for success._

Other suggestions and comments
Thank you for giving me the opportunity to provide _feedback!_

That's a Wrap!

You've made it! You now have the tools to design a favorable custom-tailored onboarding process specific to each role in your company. As we mentioned, each time you use this process, you'll begin with the same foundational structure but make adjustments that are appropriate for the position being filled. Training on specific tools and tasks will change, but orientation about company culture should always be consistent.

Throughout this book, we walked you through the seven C's of onboarding, providing tools, strategy, and structure along the way.

Here's a brief recap. If you need clarity on any part or assistance in establishing this process, or the hiring process from Book 1 in *The Team Solution Series*, don't hesitate to reach out at thejoyofpursuit.com/workwithus.

Remember, when building your onboarding process, **collaborate** with your team for a fluid onboarding process. Your leadership and department supervisors will have great insight. If your team is small or still growing, hire a competent Hiring Manager or outsource to make this a welcoming process that showcases your company while you continue to onboard champions and surpass your goals.

Keep clear lines of **communication** open between your new hire, the Hiring Manager, and department supervisors. No department should be surprised at their role in the onboarding process or when it is time to onboard a new hire. Include triggers in your process to easily transition from hiring to onboarding. For instance, notify the Tech Department that a new hire is onboarding and in which department, so they can begin preparing the proper Asset List.

Keep this book handy as you work through the process. **Challenges** will arise. If you have the right person in the role of Hiring Manager, this process will be fun for them to not only set up but implement. If you're reading this and feel apprehensive about any part of the process, it may be time to outsource or hire. If you decide to hire someone to take on your company's onboarding, have the candidate read this book or *The Team Solution Series* as a whole and make sure they understand you want this level of thorough onboarding and excellence in your company.

This is especially important as we recap **compliance**. You must hire someone who understands what compliance means and how it affects your company. If your current Hiring Manager struggles in this area, you may arrange for them to meet with agencies or legal counsel to get a better grasp on compliance and how to protect your company and all its assets.

We believe we've provided **clarity** while covering a cumbersome topic. We hope that you follow our example by setting clear expectations for your new hire, Hiring Manager, and department supervisor, as pertaining to your onboarding process.

Throughout this process, you've been connecting your new hire to the tools, systems, policies, resources, and people to help them succeed. **Connection**, as important as communication, should be part of your company culture.

By now, your new hire should have a great taste of your company's **culture**. If you didn't have a culture of excellence before this process, make implementing it a priority. While much of what is covered in onboarding includes rules, processes, and other elements that are less than exciting, remember all of this lays the foundation for an amazingly successful team who knows how to communicate and is committed to the company's Core Values and mission. When you have a team like this in place, it leads to a profitable and joyful company.

Employee engagement extends far past someone's first ninety days. Now is the time to transition to *The Retention Process* and learn valuable tools and strategies to not only keep your team together but keep them fulfilled and feeling valued for years to come.

Download The Onboarding Process Toolbox at TheJoyofPursuit.com/Onboarding

- New Hire Checklist
- Company Onboarding Checklist
- Department Checklist
- Mentor Checklist and Tips
- Icebreakers
- Team Handbook Outline
- Medical and Emergency Contact Form
- Fun Fact Form
- First-Day Schedule Example
- Goal MAP
- Onboarding ScoreCARD
- Onboarding Feedback Form

In case you missed it, we have a toolbox for hiring too. It includes the tools you need to save time, simplify steps, and strengthen your team.

Download the Hiring Process Toolbox at TheJoyOfPursuit.com/Hiring

Acknowledgments

We can't thank God enough for our grace-given gifts and abilities to break down processes to better serve others. With each book in the series, we see His hand at work using our past experiences to make an easier way for those around us. We are thankful to each other for the collaborative and complementary approach to coauthoring a series. Living our Core Value of pursuing joy daily is not something we take for granted. To all that have been supportive of this series—our families, friends, business builders—our hearts are fuller because of you.

Amanda is known both personally and professionally for her consistency, clarity, and commitment. Her grace-given gifts of practicality and focus allow her to keep an accurate perspective in life and business. She is level-headed and gives attention to the necessary priorities without distractions slowing her down. Amanda is an action-taker with a well-thought-out plan of attack in hand.

Throughout her work history, Amanda has frequently been known as the most dependable team member. She began her career with numbers and finances but grew to discover a passion for the people-side of business in Human Resources. She has a talent for identifying uniqueness in others, encouraging them to know their worth and abilities, all while gracefully holding them accountable for their actions.

Despite years of working for a publishing company, Amanda never thought she would be an author. She is now a four-time published author with an entire series for small businesses. *The Team Solution Series: HR Coaching to Grow Teams and Profit* provides more than ideas—the books are full implementation plans to guide you and your team through the employee journey. The content blends Amanda's unparalleled organizational skills with her knowledge of HR practices. Her exceptional ability to improve efficiency and processes in organizations will serve countless small business owners and strengthen their teams.

Throughout the writing and publishing process of *The Team Solution Series* (and thanks to being business partners with a top-notch book coach), Amanda knows that if she can write a book, anyone can. Together with her business partner, Brenda Haire, they created the Author Business Network, providing authors with the tools needed to successfully write, publish, market, and build a business around their books.

Amanda and her two children live at the foothills of the Smoky Mountains in Tennessee. She enjoys hiking with her kids, cooking, and gardening, especially cultivating flowers. She's known for having some of the most beautiful blooms in town. One of the greatest joys of her life is watching her children grow and guiding them to pursue their passions.

Connect with Amanda
LinkedIn.com/in/AmandaJPainter

Brenda's had over forty jobs and has been working since she was twelve. She's never been fired and is not ashamed of her work history. Brenda always worked her way up, out, and on to the next adventure. Many see this as risky and call her fearless. She would tell you that fear was always a factor—she just chose faith instead.

After being told she was a nobody by a publisher, Brenda struggled with her identity as a writer. Not one to give up, she pursued her dream and released her first book, *Save the Butter Tubs!: Discover Your Worth in a Disposable World*, in 2018.

Brenda was immediately hired by her publishing agency after her book was released, and she went on to become the president of the company. An entrepreneur at heart, once again she left on top and now uses her experience to serve individuals and small businesses around the world as the CEO and cofounder of Joy of Pursuit. Brenda created the Author Business Network with her business partner,

Amanda Painter, and together they help authors build businesses around their books.

As a speaker, Brenda shares keynotes and workshops that transform audiences. Whether she is speaking about purpose, publishing, or small business, her deepest desire is to help you shine your light by operating in your grace-given gifts. She considers herself a moved soul—so moved by her encounters with God that she can't help but move in response. She wants the same for you—to encounter God in a way that you can't help but live a life worthy of your calling.

She and her hubs (as she lovingly refers to him on social media), Darren, are both military veterans. They enjoy hiking and chasing waterfalls across the United States and live in Texas with their beautifully blended and expanding family.

Connect with Brenda
Facebook.com/BrendaHaire
Instagram.com/BrendaAHaire
LinkedIn.com/in/Brenda Haire

Empower Your Team
Elevate Your Business

» Strategies to Find and Keep Top Talent.

» Techniques that Boost Employee Engagement and Reduce Turnover.

» Tools to Ensure Smooth Transitions and Protect Your Business.

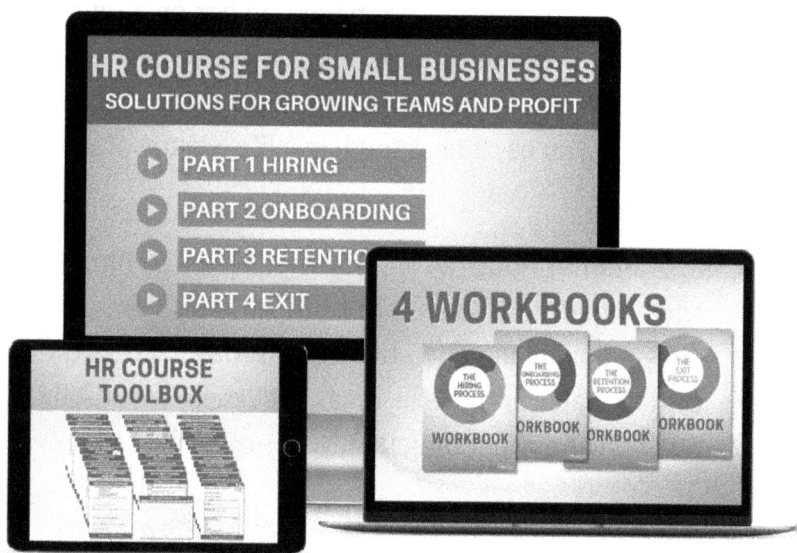

HR COURSE FOR SMALL BUSINESSES
SOLUTIONS FOR GROWING TEAMS AND PROFIT

▶ PART 1 HIRING

▶ PART 2 ONBOARDING

▶ PART 3 RETENTIO

▶ PART 4 EXIT

4 WORKBOOKS

HR COURSE
TOOLBOX

THE HIRING PROCESS WORKBOOK

THE ONBOARDING PROCESS ORKBOOK

THE RETENTION PROCESS ORKBOOK

THE EXIT PROCESS ORKBOOK

Unlock the Full Potential of Your Team » ENROLL NOW

TheJoyofPursuit.com/HR-Course

Revolutionize Your Business
with Our HR Consulting Services

Receive Exclusive HR Insights, Industry News, and Best Practices Straight to Your Inbox.

CUT THE CHAOS

One email per month to take you and your business from tired and busy to thriving and productive!

Try it today

Tools.TheJoyOfPursuit.com/CutTheChaos

Take the next step in creating a culture of growth and fulfillment of purpose.

COMPLETE THE
TEAM SOLUTION SERIES

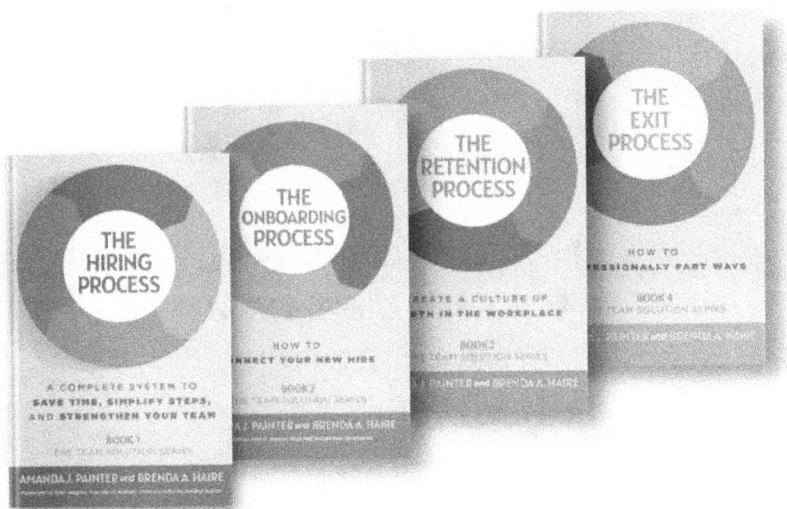

THE
HIRING
PROCESS

A COMPLETE SYSTEM TO
SAVE TIME, SIMPLIFY STEPS,
AND STRENGTHEN YOUR TEAM

BOOK 1
THE TEAM SOLUTION SERIES

AMANDA J. PAINTER and BRENDA A. HAIRE

THE
ONBOARDING
PROCESS

HOW TO
CONNECT YOUR NEW HIRE

BOOK 2
THE TEAM SOLUTION SERIES

A.J. PAINTER and BRENDA A. HAIRE

THE
RETENTION
PROCESS

CREATE A CULTURE OF
GROWTH IN THE WORKPLACE

BOOK 3
THE TEAM SOLUTION SERIES

A.J. PAINTER and BRENDA A. HAIRE

THE
EXIT
PROCESS

HOW TO
PROFESSIONALLY PART WAYS

BOOK 4
THE TEAM SOLUTION SERIES

A.J. PAINTER and BRENDA A. HAIRE

TheJoyOfPursuit.com/Books

Transform Your Workplace

Build a Custom Workshop for Your Team

Higher Productivity
Efficient Meetings
Lower Turnover
Engaged Employees
Cohesive Leadership Team

It's Time to Create a
Joyful Workplace
for YOU and Your Team!

TheJoyOfPursuit.com/Workshops

Buy in Bulk

for Your Human Resource Team,
Directors, or Leadership Team

TheJoyofPursuit.com/Books